THE 108 NA...

Ashima Singh

Series Editor: Shalini Saran

VIKING

VIKING

Penguin Books India (P) Ltd., 11 Community Centre, Panchsheel Park, New Delhi 110 017, India

Penguin Books Ltd., 80 Strand, London WC2R 0RL, UK

Penguin Putnam Inc., 375 Hudson Street, New York, NY 10014, USA

Penguin Books Australia Ltd., 250 Camberwell Road, Camberwell, Victoria 3124, Australia

Penguin Books Canada Ltd., 10 Alcorn Avenue, Suite 300, Toronto, Ontario, M4V 3B2, Canada

Penguin Books (NZ) Ltd., Cnr Rosedale and Airborne Roads, Albany, Auckland, New Zealand

First published in Viking by Penguin Books India 2002

Copyright © Ashima Singh 2002

Typeset in Venetian by S.R. Enterprises, New Delhi

Printed at Saurabh Print-O-Pack, Noida

वक्रतुण्ड महाकाय सूर्यकोटि समप्रभ।
निर्विघ्नम् कुरुमेदेव सर्वकार्येषु सर्वदा।।

Vakratunda mahaakaaya sooryakoti samaprabha
Nirvighnam kurumedeva sarvakaaryeshu sarvadaa.

You of the curved trunk and massive body with the brilliance and light of a million suns, bless my endeavours and remove all obstacles that may hinder my path. Bless me forever.

AUTHOR'S NOTE

Spiritual growth is independent of religious beliefs. Religion and rituals can serve as guides and they can help discipline the seeker but the actual process of spiritual growth is totally non-religious. The inner self needs to be in tune with the Absolute Divine Self for the optimum utilization of inner forces. Spiritual growth is related to the refining of the cognitive perceptions of the entire range of emotions, expectations, desires and experiences. This then makes us aware enough to realize that we are manifestations of the same Absolute Source of all creation.

INTRODUCTION

Lord Ganesha

Who is Ganesha, the deity with the body of a man and the head of an elephant? Who or what are we invoking? Lord Ganesha has been worshipped for centuries as one who protects the devotee from devastation and also as one who bestows good harvests. Ganesha is perceived as a lovable god, benevolent, auspicious and invoked at the start of any venture. But what does he truly symbolize?

While Ganesha is propitiated mainly as the remover of obstacles, he is also the most important energy being to invoke. This is because Ganesha is *Gana-eesha*, the lord (*eesha*) of the celestial hordes (*gana*). Gana also means 'category', 'the countless' or 'the numbered'.

In purely spiritual terms, which transcend religion and mythology, Ganesha is one of innumerable channels of energy which emanate from the unified field of cosmic energy. He is symbolic of that energy which enables us to overcome obstacles related to our physical and emotional selves. He cleanses us, so that we may touch higher realms of consciousness.

Every energy which exists in the cosmos exists in our physical body and affects our psycho-spiritual structure (*yathaa pindey, tathaa brahmaandey*). The human being is truly a microcosm of the cosmos; the celestial hordes are elementals or nature spirits and they are reflected in our body as countless cells. By invoking Ganesha we understand, alter, heal and align our cellular structure and hence make our bodies more receptive to divine grace.

Invoking Ganesha

To invoke the divine within and to know the purpose of life, we have to know the life force within us, the *aatmaa, rooh* or soul, which is beyond the body. This happens with inward growth which, in turn, develops through the refining of the spirit, the evolution of the intellect and through self-awareness which is the faculty which allows us to be a witness to our states of mind, to discern between the different levels of consciousness and ultimately dwell in a state of higher awareness.

Most of us are caught up in our physical and emotional existences. Those whose finer intellect has reached above a certain level, those who are ready to sift all knowledge and draw the essence for self-purification and enlightenment through experience, are able to cross all barriers. They are able to rise towards the goal of pure consciousness.

In ancient times, spiritual growth was seen as being linked to austerity. But it is possible to live in comfort, to have wealth and still be spiritually aware. To go beyond the body we have to be aware of the body and not neglect physical existence. The body is that instrument which contains the life form known as the *jeeva aatmaa*. The purpose of refining our energies is to reach out to the *param aatmaa*, for total integration with God. Even though this is the goal of every religion, religion per se can only discipline and guide the seeker. The process itself is totally non-religious.

To invoke divine grace with attention and awareness is a profound step on the path which leads to spiritual knowledge. Traditionally, there are three paths open to the seeker of spiritual knowledge—*gyaan*, *bhakti* and *karma* and the three associated activities are *tantra*, *yantra* and *mantra*. Tantra is the actualization of dormant physical energy; yantra is a device or instrument geometrically designed to contain focal energy; mantra uses the power of the mind to impel the energy force field around the physical body through sound vibrations.

Chanting a mantra or the name of the divine is an acknowledged practice for getting connected to that which is being invoked. The act of chanting has its own value, for it creates a force field of particular sound energies. The sound vibrations which emanate in the process of chanting, in turn, permeate the energy bodies, both of the listener and of the one who is chanting. If both energy bodies are sensitive and receptive, the effect is deeply beneficial. Different energy centres in the body relate to different sounds and tonal variations created by the chanting. When the energies of the body and the mind are integrated, then there is the realization that spiritual knowledge is available to the seeker.

The number 108 is common both to prayer beads and invocations. It is in fact a symbolic invocation of the cosmos. There are twenty-seven constellations or *nakshatras* in our galaxy. They are called constellations because they are constant and fixed corridors of energy. Each constellation has four sections. When 108 names are chanted sound vibrations are sent out in all directions and resonate back from all 108 corridors of energy. This resonance balances the vibrations all around the bio-plasmic energy body. Energy and matter are interchangeable. This change can happen in two ways—either by direct transference of energy from a higher energy body like a *guru* or healer, or by refining and integrating one's own energies so as to be able to reach out to the source of all energy.

Ganesha and Energy

The gross or physical body is surrounded by the energy field of the auric or bio-plasmic body. In this auric body are located centres of energy known as *chakras*. Chakras are whorls of energy and whatever we receive from the environment and the Supreme Source is routed through these chakras to the physical body. Both these bodies are interpenetrable. From the base of the spine to the top of the head there are seven major chakras. Located at the base of the spine is the root chakra or *mooladhara chakra* which is the base for our structural body and for the multiplication of cells for healthy blood. The navel chakra is the energy centre through which we nourish and regenerate the body. The solar plexus is located in the diaphragm, in the area below the heart. This chakra is the centre of all lower emotions like anger, fear, avarice, lust and hate. The heart chakra symbolizes the beginning of the awareness of higher emotions and the letting go of lower emotions. The throat chakra is the centre of creativity. The *ajna* or master chakra is located between the eyebrows. It controls and energizes the pituitary gland and is called the master chakra because it disciplines and directs all the major chakras and the endocrine system. The crown chakra is often referred to as the one with the thousand petals. In the centre of this chakra is the pineal gland and at the top of the head, is the *antahkarna*, the spiritual cord which acts as a receptor for the inflow of higher energy.

Ganesha, as lord of our cellular structure is the lord of the mooladhara chakra, which also carries the genetic code. A healthy and vital root chakra leads to the production of healthy cells, and consequently, physical well-being. Ganesha is also propitiated as the starting point of the ascent to awareness, as the one who causes that energy to rise up which leads the seeker to a union with the divine.

There are specific mantras and invocations for each deity or energy being. Over the centuries, devotees of Ganesha have used epithets in praise of, but also out of love for, Ganesha. Each epithet is a revelation of the divine. Between its literal and symbolic meanings there exist many layers of interpretation related to mythology and religion. However, the essence of each epithet is beyond both religion and mythology. It is a pointer to the divine and to our own spiritual selves.

Origins

The origin of Ganesha as we know him lies in the Rig Vedic deity Ganapati-Brahmanaspati. This deity was red in colour and carried weapons, amongst which the battle-axe was the most important. He was always in the company of a group of singers and dancers. He destroyed the enemies of the gods and protected his devotees. He was also worshipped as a scribe and a god of agriculture whose blessings brought forth a good harvest. An elephant-headed deity was also worshipped in ancient Afghanistan, Tibet, Central Asia, Mongolia and Japan. According to a Vedic verse on creation it was Ganapati who blew the conch from which emanated the sound *Aum*. As with so many other deities, this elephant-headed deity, too, was assimilated into the Hindu pantheon. The elephant was considered especially auspicious by the Aryans and in time Ganesha, as the deity came to be known, was accepted as a Hindu god and legitimized in myths.

There are accounts of Ganesha in the *Shiva, Matsya, Padma, Varaaha, Skanda, Linga* and *Brahmavaivarta Puranas*, in the *Minor* or *Upa Puranas* and the *Ganesha* and *Mudgala Puranas*.

Legends about Ganesha's Birth

There are many variations in each of the myths related to the birth of Ganesha. In one he is the *manas-putra*, the 'mind-born' child who emerged from the brilliance of

Shiva's consciousness when the gods and demigods, harassed by demons, begged for Shiva's protection.

Shiva gave the boy the head of an elephant and armed him with a trident. Parvati was delighted and accepted the boy as her own. She even ordained that no endeavour, human or divine, would be successful without a prayer to this child. And Shiva proclaimed him to be the leader of his ganas, or celestial hordes.

In another version of this myth, Parvati was resentful that such a handsome boy was created without her involvement. Such was her anger that she willed his head to turn into that of an elephant. But once she saw the elephant-headed boy she was overwhelmed with love for him. Ganesha, she said, was to be worshipped first and foremost, before invoking any other energy or embarking upon any venture.

The *Shiva Purana* contains one of the most popular myths related to the birth of Ganesha. It is said that Parvati's handmaidens, Jaya and Vijaya, complained to the goddess that while Shiva's ganas were subservient to him, the ladies could not get the ganas to obey them. They pleaded with the goddess for servants of their own. Parvati considered this plea worthwhile and resolved to act upon it. As Shiva entered her apartment as and when he wished, she often suffered from a lack of privacy. So she too desired to have somebody who would serve her alone and never stray from her behest. Thus from her *ubtan* (unguents) she created a youth—handsome, strong, valiant and large. She adorned him with beautiful clothes and ornaments and told him he was her son. She armed him with a stick and posted him as her gatekeeper. She instructed him to forbid any person to enter her apartment. The youth promised to obey her command and stood guard as Parvati went in to bathe. Shortly thereafter Shiva arrived, filled with eagerness, to meet his wife. The boy stopped him and said his mother's permission was needed before allowing any person to enter. Shiva was enraged. He called the boy foolish and wicked and declared that he was Shiva himself. The boy ignored it all and beat Shiva with his staff. Shiva at once summoned his ganas, who questioned the boy. The fearless boy in turn, questioned them. The arrogant ganas conferred with one another, expressed their desire not to kill the boy and requested him to leave. But the boy refused. When the ganas complained to Shiva he said, 'Are you eunuchs that you stand there helpless?' They rushed back to the boy who then struck them with his stick. This time, Shiva ridiculed his ganas, calling them impotent wretches'.

In the meantime, Parvati had sent her maid to enquire about the uproar outside. The maid found out what had happened and reported it to Parvati. The goddess thought about the situation, and then decided to let the boy do as he had been bid. Hearing of his mother's decision, the boy became bolder and stronger. He told the ganas that he carried out the orders of Parvati just as they did those of Shiva. None, he declared, could enter either humbly or forcibly. When this was reported to Shiva, he felt it may not be proper to force an entry. But neither would it do to be humble, thought the great lord, for then it would be rumoured that Shiva was subservient to his wife. So it was decided that a battle would be fought, between a strong army and a boy. But such was the boy's strength that he routed the ganas. Urged by the sage Narada, Vishnu and Brahma came to pay obeisance to Shiva. The great lord apprised them of the situation, and it was decided that Brahma and the sages should approach the boy. But their plea for peace fell on deaf ears. The boy took up his club and even tugged at Brahma's beard and moustache. Shiva was even more enraged when he heard this. He summoned all the goblins and ghosts and Indra's *yakshas*. A huge battle ensued, and the earth and all the oceans quaked and the planets and stars trembled in the sky. To aid her son, Parvati created two forms of Shakti; one swallowed all the weapons hurled at the boy and then threw them back, the other became lightning. Vishnu and Shiva then joined the formidable battle. It was while the boy was fighting Vishnu, that Shiva cut off his head with his trident.

There was great rejoicing amongst the ganas. But now it was Parvati's turn to be enraged, and the wrath of Shakti was awesome. She threatened to wreak destruction upon heaven and earth and with such ferocity that even Shiva was fearful.

Then Shiva and the other gods paid obeisance to Parvati, whom they hailed as Primordial Shakti, the eternal cause of creation and its sustaining power. Parvati was pleased and became filled with compassion. She asked that her son be brought back to life.

The gods conferred amongst themselves. Shiva sent his ganas to find the first living creature with its head facing north, the auspicious direction. It turned out to be an elephant. Shiva placed this elephant head on the severed trunk and resuscitated the boy, who woke up as if from sleep, handsome, elephant-faced and red-complexioned.

Parvati was delighted by his radiance. She gave him clothes and ornaments, and embraced and blessed him and commanded that he be worshipped before all the gods.

Then Brahma, Vishnu and Shiva ordained that he would be worshipped in all the three worlds like themselves and that he would be the remover of obstacles and the bestower of success. Shiva then proclaimed him the presiding officer of all his ganas. Thus the boy was named Ganesha.

These myths related to the birth of Ganesha are amongst the most popular. There are others too. They all have two common factors: the human head of the boy is replaced by that of an elephant, and the boy is named Ganesha, the lord of the ganas.

The Destruction of Tripuraasura

Shiva once forgot what he himself had decreed—that Ganesha be worshipped at the start of any endeavour. It happened when he set off to destroy the demon Tripuraasura.

According to the *Shiva Purana*, Shiva's second son, Skanda (Kartikeya), was created to destroy the demon Taraka. He accomplished the task. But the demon had three sons who began to perform penance to gain strength and refuge. Brahma, whom they propitiated, granted them a boon. They asked that none other than Shiva could kill them and they asked for three cities in which they could find refuge.

Brahma created three beautiful cities, one for each of the demons. However, in time these demons became so powerful, that the gods became uneasy. So Shiva decided to destroy them.

In one version of the myth, the nail in the wheel of Shiva's chariot broke and the chariot stalled, just as the great lord was about to set forth. In another version, as Shiva stood poised with his deadly weapon, Ganesha stood before him, obstructing his path. Shiva was furious in both cases, until Ganesha reminded him of his promise to Parvati—that he be worshipped at the start of any endeavour. Shiva complied and attained success in his mission.

Ganesha Loses His Tusk

Parashurama was one of the incarnations of Vishnu, born on earth to destroy erring and unjust rulers. Shiva gave him the divine axe, Parashu, and with it, Parashurama was able to accomplish his mission.

When he came to Mount Kailash to offer thanks to Shiva, he was refused entry by Ganesha, who insisted he needed permission to do so. Parashurama thought otherwise; when Ganesha persisted in his refusal, Parashurama struck his tusk with the axe, breaking it. Later, Parashurama had to seek the forgiveness and the blessings of Ganesha.

In another version of this myth, when Parashurama insisted on entering Shiva's chambers, Ganesha wrapped his trunk around him and hurled him round and round till he was unconscious. When Parashurama regained his senses he threw his axe at Ganesha who, recognizing it as Shiva's invincible weapon, let it fall on one tusk.

Ganesha's Mount

Ganesha's broken tusk is also linked to the slaying of the demon Gajamukhaasura. The demon had, after severe penance, obtained invincible powers from Shiva. But thereafter he provoked the wrath of the gods, who in turn approached Ganesha for help. Ganesha, aware of the power of Shiva's boon, realized he could not kill the demon. So he broke his right tusk, hurled it at the demon cursing him to turn into a mouse which he then rode.

Ganesha's mouse, a demon in one myth, is the Gandharva Krauncha in another. Indra turned Krauncha into a rat because he insulted the sage Vaamadeva. The cursed rat then entered the *ashram* of the sage Paraashara in order to destroy it. The sage then prayed to Ganesha who brought the rat under his control.

Ganesha the Scribe

Ganesha is believed to have used his broken tusk to write the Mahabharata. It is said that Veda Vyasa, disturbed by the misinterpretation of the *Vedas*, sought to compile all their knowledge in a single epic. So he wove the wisdom of the *Vedas* into a story comprised of more than 100,000 verses. But he needed a scribe to write down the epic. Brahma told the sage that Ganesha alone could accomplish this task. Ganesha then agreed to be the scribe on the condition that Vyasa would dictate his epic without a pause. Vyasa countered this rather difficult condition by stipulating one of his own—that Ganesha should write only with complete understanding.

So, in the course of composing the epic Vyasa would, every now and then, dictate a complex and difficult *shloka*. As Ganesha pondered over the meanings of these shlokas, Vyasa would use this time to compose the following verses.

Ganesha's Wisdom

Once, Shiva and Parvati were playing with their beloved sons, Ganesha and Skanda. The divine couple had received a fruit from the gods which contained the nectar of Supreme Knowledge. Both the sons wanted this first, so the parents told them that the first one who circled the world three times would obtain the fruit.

Skanda immediately flew off on his peacock to circumnavigate the earth. But Ganesha pondered over the impediment created by his size and the fact that his vehicle was a rat. However, using his intelligence, he circled his parents three times and demanded the fruit. Then he explained to his puzzled parents that he had in effect circled the earth, (its oceans, seven continents and the vast jungles) for they, his parents, contained the whole universe within them. They were the whole world to him. Shiva and Parvati were amazed and pleased by their son's intelligence and granted him the fruit.

Ganesha and Kubera

Kubera, the treasurer of the gods, once invited the child Ganesha for a meal. Ganesha ate the food, the platters, the furniture, even Kubera's capital. He then threatened to devour Kubera himself. Kubera pleaded to Shiva for mercy. Shiva then gave his son a fistful of roasted grain and immediately Ganesha's appetite was satiated.

Iconography

Over the centuries, these and other myths related to Ganesha have found expression in the complex iconography of Ganesha images.

He is portrayed both sitting and standing and sometimes in a dancing posture for Ganesha is also Nrittya Kovidam, the perfect dancer, the one who dances in sheer joy. He is shown with two, four, six, eight, ten or sixteen arms.

There are thirty-two forms of Ganesha and each one symbolizes a different aspect of the deity. He is depicted as a beloved child, a warrior, a symbol of power and achievement, the protector of the weak, the bestower of success and boons, the one who grants *moksha*, the remover of sorrow, the twice-born one, the golden one, the creator, the *tantric* deity, the single-tusked one, the one who acts promptly, Dhundiganapati of Kashi, the god with two or three faces; the dancer, the great *yogi* and the one who rides a lion. According to the most common image, he bears, in his hands, stalks of wheat or sugarcane, weapons, objects used in worship, agricultural implements, fruits and flowers and symbols of protection, wisdom and blessings.

We see images of Ganesha everywhere; his auspicious name is used, as a symbol of prosperity, for textile mills, brands of food, stationery, milk and on workshops and food stalls. On Ganesha Chathurthi, celebrated with great enthusiasm in Maharashtra, immense and colourful images of the elephant-headed deity are taken out in procession and immersed in the sea.

The explanations which follow each of the epithets of Ganesha in this book are not bound by religion; they are related to energy—the cleansing, purifying and revitalizing of energy for attaining a true understanding of one's spiritual self. This interpretation of the 108 names of Ganesha will, I hope, impart a finer understanding of the vital divine energy which he symbolizes.

★ ★ ★ ★ ★

ॐ विश्वरदाय नमः
Aum Vishvaradaaya Namah

Salutations to the benefactor of the universe

Ganesha's energies are all-pervading. He is invoked as
the power which benefits the entire universe, and whose
benign force touches man at all three levels—physical,
emotional and spiritual.

ॐ विघ्नेशाय नमः

Aum Vighneshaaya Namah

Salutations to the lord who governs obstacles

Expectations, anxieties, disappointments and fears born out of desire and attachment to material possessions are the real obstacles on the path to happiness. They obstruct the natural flow of energy affecting vital organs in the body. The wise man is one who experiences the whole range of emotions but sees himself as their master rather than their slave. Mental obstacles are removed by invoking, understanding and becoming aware of the energies which Ganesha symbolizes. In mythology, Ganesha as Vighnaraj overcame attachment and desire.

ॐ विश्वचक्षुषे नमः

Aum Vishvachakshushey Namah

Salutations to the eye of the universe

Ganesha is invoked as that energy which watches over everything happening around us and also enables us to be a witness to it. He is 'the spirit which enables the eye to see, but needs no eye to see.' (*Katho Upanishad*)

ॐ जगत्प्रभवे नमः
Aum Jagatprabhavey Namah

Salutations to the supreme creative source of the universe

Ganesha symbolizes that supreme energy which dwells at the very source of creation. This is immeasurable, infinite, inexhaustible divine energy which flows continuously as a benign force, and is available to all desirous of receiving it.

ॐ हिरण्यरूपाय नमः

Aum Hiranyaroopaaya Namah

Salutations to the one who is pure, dazzling, golden energy

Ganesha is the lord of our cellular structure and hence of our basic existence. He is synonymous with the nurturing or golden energy which is pure, bright and life-bestowing, like the light of the sun.

ॐ सर्वात्मने नमः

Aum Sarvaatmaney Namah

Salutations to the all-pervading soul

We are essentially spiritual beings going through human experiences, the emotional intensity of which leads us to an awareness of the existence of higher consciousness. 'All living beings are permeated with the lord whose form is one, yet manifold; whose essence is one, yet diverse; who is tenuous yet vast; discernible yet indiscernible; root of the world, yet composed of the world.' (*Vishnu Purana*)

ॐ ज्ञानरूपाय नमः

Aum Gyaanaroopaaya Namah

Salutations to the one who is knowledge incarnate

To know Ganesha is to know oneself, because knowledge of Ganesha is only attained through knowledge of one's own self. Knowledge is awareness and awareness is the ability to discern.

ॐ जगन्मनाय नमः

Aum Jaganmanaaya Namah

Salutations to the one who is universal consciousness

'Supreme consciousness is like the brilliant radiance of a large lamp, situated inside a pot with many holes, which spreads its light externally. If supreme consciousness were to be perceived as an immense source of light, then each living being is like a repository of a ray of light from that source.' (*Brahma Meditations*)

ॐ ऊर्ध्वरेतसे नमः

Aum Oordhvaretasey Namah

Salutations to the one with ascending energies

There are seven major chakras or energy centres in the bio-plasmic body (see Introduction pp. 5–6). Ganesha is the lord of the root chakra—the lord of our basic existence. His energy is constantly ascending towards higher chakras and heightened states of awareness.

ॐ महाबाहवे नमः
Aum Mahaabaahavey Namah

**Salutations to the one with the
all-encompassing embrace**

Ganesha's massive arms are a symbol of the immense
reach of his energy. This benevolent energy, in its
compassion, encompasses all that exists.

ॐ अमेयाय नमः
Aum Ameyaaya Namah

**Salutations to the one who is infinite
and immeasurable**

Ganesha is symbolic of energy which is omnipresent
and all-pervading. This energy is beyond measure, and
is a force which cannot be quantified, for it never
diminishes even as it continually nourishes our souls.

ॐ अमितविक्रमाय नमः

Aum Amitavikramaaya Namah

Salutations to the one with unlimited prowess and valour

When invoked, Ganesha can impart boundless protective energy, as well as energy which empowers our desire to explore the potential of the human spirit. The sheer size of Ganesha's form represents a solid mass of energy which symbolizes strength as well as the ability to transform that strength into pure energy.

ॐ वेदवेद्याय नमः

Aum Vedavedyaaya Namah

Salutations to one who is understood through the *Vedas*

Veda means knowledge. In mythology, Brahma was created by the combined energies of Vishnu and Shiva. Brahma appeared, bearing in his hands the four *Vedas*. The *Vedas* are a guide to a perfect existence, and through their knowledge it is possible to understand the immensity of Ganesha's energies.

ॐ महाकालाय नमः

Aum Mahaakaalaaya Namah

Salutations to the one who is time itself

'The past and future, and all sacred knowledge and austerity issue out of time. The earth and waters were produced from time, as was the rising, setting, burning sun, and the wind. Through time, the earth is vast, through time the eye perceives; mind, breath and name in time are comprehended.' (*Atharva Veda*)

ॐ विद्यानिधये नमः

Aum Vidyaanidhaye Namah

Salutations to the treasure trove of knowledge

'Ganesha shines like a jewel of pure knowledge whose coming forth reveals the nature of true being amidst the forms produced in false being. He gives direct knowledge to those who turn to him.' (*Brahma Meditations*)

ॐ अनामयाय नमः

Aum Anaamayaaya Namah

Salutations to the wholesome one

Physical existence is linked to, and is dependent on, the strength of the root chakra which resonates with the energies of the earth. This epithet expresses the wholesomeness of the energy which Ganesha, as lord of the root chakra, symbolizes.

ॐ सर्वज्ञाय नमः

Aum Sarvagyaaya Namah

Salutations to the omniscient one

Ganesha is a reservoir of pure knowledge which a devotee can draw upon to guide and nourish his evolving consciousness.

'One can forever dip into this knowledge—and while the individual's knowledge is enriched Ganesha's reservoir never gets depleted.' (*Katho Upanishad*)

ॐ सर्वगाय नमः

Aum Sarvagaaya Namah

Salutations to the omnipresent one

Ganesha emerges from pure consciousness and since all
creation is within the field of pure consciousness, Ganesha
is everywhere. 'The self is omnipresent, without a body,
without a shape, whole, pure, all-knowing, far-shining,
self-depending, all-transcending.' (*Isha Upanishad*)

ॐ शांताय नमः

Aum Shaantaaya Namah

Salutations to the one who is free of excesses

Ganesha is symbolic of energy that does not indulge in
the excess of any emotion or passion. While it is important
to experience both emotion and passion it is equally
important not to overindulge in either but to remain a
witness to it all, and strike a balance within in order to
attain peace.

ॐ चित्तेश्वराय नमः
Aum Chitteshvaraaya Namah

Salutations to the lord of our consciousness

Chiti is awareness. Experiences take us through different levels of awareness. Chitteshvara is the lord who helps us explore the different levels of awareness and perpetuates the expansion of consciousness.

ॐ विगतज्वराय नमः
Aum Vigatajvaraaya Namah

Salutations to the one without stress or grief

Ganesha is the one who knows how to detach himself
from negative emotions like hurt and grief because he
has understood both their cause and effect. He does not
get disturbed or rattled by such emotions because, as
pure knowledge, he has transcended them.

ॐ विश्वमूर्तये नमः
Aum Vishvamoortaye Namah

Salutations to the universe incarnate

Ganesha is the tangible life force which permeates every living creature, the one who exists in all life forms. The entire universe, from Brahma to a blade of grass, are his forms.

ॐ अमेयात्मने नमः

Aum Ameyaatmaney Namah

Salutations to the boundless soul

The individual soul vibrates directly in consonance with the supreme soul, which is immeasurable. 'The self or universal soul knows all; it is not born, it does not die, it is not the effect of any cause; it is eternal, self-existent, imperishable, ancient.' (*Katho Upanishad*)

ॐ विश्वाधाराय नमः

Aum Vishvaadhaaraaya Namah

Salutations to the sustainer of the universe

Ganesha extends his help to all and everything that exists. His energy is the very foundation and sustenance of all creation, both animate and inanimate.

ॐ सनातनाय नमः

Aum Sanaatanaaya Namah

Salutations to the one who is continual

The eternal spirit neither comes nor goes. It is always there, without beginning or end. It is changeless, yet causes change all around. The universal spirit is perpetual consciousness, bliss and truth.

ॐ सामगाय नमः

Aum Saamagaaya Namah

Salutations to the embodiment of harmony

As Saamaga, Ganesha is the epitome of harmony. He is that effortless song of equality, proportion and balance, which symbolizes the unity of the self.

ॐ प्रियाय नमः

Aum Priyaaya Namah

Salutations to the one who is love itself

By invoking the purity of being that is Ganesha we experience the immense force of the flow of love. In its purest form, love is compassion. The more we become aware of love as compassion, the more it flows our way from the divine. The more compassion we extend, the more we experience and generate it.

ॐ सत्त्वाधाराय नमः
Aum Sattvaadhaaraaya Namah

**Salutations to the supporter of the
quintessence of all beings**

Ganesha is symbolic of strength, vitality and qualities of
purity and goodness. The path to awakening is the
realization that our spiritual self is one with the universal
spirit and with all that is pure and continuous.

ॐ सुराधीशाय नमः
Aum Suraadheeshaaya Namah

Salutations to the one who is revered by the gods

Yathaa pindey, tathaa brahmaandey. Every energy that exists in the cosmos exists in the human form. Here, Ganesha is referred to as the one who is praised by all heavenly beings. The cells in our body, which are the microcosmic counterpart of the heavenly beings, also praise him.

ॐ समस्तसाक्षिणे नमः

Aum Samastasaakshiney Namah

Salutations to the one who witnesses all

Being in possession of knowledge and being aware makes us see everything in a larger perspective. Ganesha is pure awareness that witnesses all. 'He witnesses the universe from the outside though it arose within himself.' (*Brahma Meditations*)

ॐ निर्द्वन्द्वाय नमः

Aum Nirdvandvaaya Namah

Salutations to the one without conflict

The one whose energies are totally integrated, harmonious, confluent and in consonance with one another, is the one who knows inherent harmony and poise. 'When all the knots of the heart are destroyed even while a man is still alive, then a mortal becomes immortal.' (*Katho Upanishad*)

ॐ निर्लोकाय नमः

Aum Nirlokaaya Namah

Salutations to the one who does not belong to one realm alone

The seven realms of existence, ranging from the gross physical to the supramental levels, symbolize the seven levels of energy reflected in the seven major chakras. Ganesha, as the lord of our entire cellular structure, spans the various realms of existence.

ॐ अमोघविक्रमाय नमः

Aum Amoghavikramaaya Namah

Salutations to the invincible one

Ganesha's energy is indestructible. 'It is infallible. It cannot be decimated. It is without change.' (*Mahanirvana Tantra*)

ॐ पुण्याय नमः

Aum Punyaaya Namah

Salutations to the virtuous one

Ganesha is virtue itself. He evokes all that is good, pure, sacred and glorious in human thought and behaviour. He brings out the inherent goodness in man.

ॐ निर्मलाय नम:

Aum Nirmalaaya Namah

Salutations to the chaste one

Ganesha is clear, chaste, radiant light. These are the qualities of the energy which Ganesha symbolizes—that energy which is entirely devoid of impurity.

ॐ कामदाय नमः

Aum Kaamadaaya Namah

Salutations to the one who fulfils all desires

There are seven types of desire—the desires for security, procreation, longevity, sharing, knowledge, self-realization and union with the divine. These correspond with the seven colours of light, the seven major chakras and the seven levels of existence. Kaamada Ganesha fulfils all worldly desires and propels us towards higher levels of existence.

ॐ कांतिदाय नमः

Aum Kantidaaya Namah

Salutations to the one who bestows radiance

The word *guru* means the dispellor (*ru*) of darkness (*gu*).
Ganesha is invoked as the one who dispels the darkness
of ignorance and reveals the glory of the goodness of the
inner being.

ॐ कामरूपिणे नमः

Aum Kaamaroopiney Namah

Salutations to the one who can assume any form

Ganesha symbolizes the one who sees no duality, who can merge his consciousness with any life form—plant, animal or human and become that form. He is the divine presence in every form of life.

ॐ कामपोषिणे नमः

Aum Kaamaposhiney Namah

Salutations to the one who nurtures our desires

Ganesha reflects our latent desires, brings them to light
and nurtures them. Experience adds to the growth of
our perception hence the act of nurturing our desires
also helps us to let go of them. 'Though himself devoid
of senses, he is the illuminator of all senses and their
power.' (*Mahanirvana Tantra*)

ॐ कमलाक्षाय नमः
Aum Kamalaakshaaya Namah

Salutations to the lotus-eyed one

The lotus is the symbol of purity and of untainted
beauty, as it emerges unsullied by its surroundings.
Ganesha's eyes are soft, gentle and compassionate—
reflecting his inner luminosity.

ॐ गजाननाय नमः

Aum Gajaananaaya Namah

Salutations to the elephant-faced one

Ganesha's elephant face is a symbol of wisdom and power. Its size is also a symbol of intellectual prowess and expanded consciousness. In ancient times, the elephant was the auspicious mark of prosperity. As Gajaanana, Ganesha subdued the demons of avarice and greed. The word *gaja* also has a more profound connotation. *Ga* is linked to *gati*, the ultimate goal towards which all creation, knowingly or unknowingly, is moving. *Ja* is the root of *janma*—birth or origin. *Gaja* therefore symbolizes God from whom all worlds have emerged and towards whom they are progressing in an ultimate union.

ॐ सुमुखाय नमः
Aum Sumukhaaya Namah

Salutations to the one with the beautiful face

Ganesha's face reflects the experience of awareness. It also reflects the experience of a profound consciousness and brings out the beauty of his inner qualities.

ॐ शर्मदाय नमः
Aum Sharmadaaya Namah

Salutations to the bestower of happiness

Shrm and *Sham* are the *beej* (seed) sounds chanted during *Pranayama* for generating quietitude and tranquillity. As Sharmada, Ganesha is the bestower of *that* happiness which is brought about by the tranquillity of the mind.

ॐ मूषकाधिपवाहनाय नमः
Aum Mooshakaadhipavaahanaaya Namah

Salutations to the one who rides a big mouse

The word *mooshaka* stems from the word *moosh* which means to steal. The mouse enters with stealth and goes unnoticed. Here, the mouse symbolizes petty desires which also enter unnoticed and make the mind restless. It is this restlessness which prevents us from focussing and channelizing our energies. This aspect of Ganesha makes us aware of how our inner equilibrium can be disturbed.

ॐ शुद्धाय नमः

Aum Shuddhaaya Namah

Salutations to the sanctified one

Shuddh is that which is sanctified, that which is the very
nectar of life. It is the innate quality of that energy which
provides vitality and potency to our being.

ॐ दीर्घतुंडाय नमः
Aum Deerghatundaaya Namah

Salutations to the one with the long trunk

The long trunk symbolizes the deft use of a sensory organ. The elephant uses its long trunk for purposes as varied as lifting a log of wood, plucking a blade of grass and drinking water.

ॐ श्रीपतये नमः
Aum Shreepatayey Namah

Salutations to the lord of immense prosperity and plenty

Ganesha's *laddoos*, fragrant and sweet, symbolize *sattva*, the most refined state of pure consciousness. This refined state generates a feeling of the richness of possibilities in every sphere, just as space contains infinite possibilities of growth and supports the fecundity of nature in every form.

ॐ अनंताय नमः

Aum Anantaaya Namah

Salutations to the unending one

'He is without change, he is self-existent and ever the same, serene and above all attributes. He beholds and is the witness of all that is, and is the self of everything that is. He, the eternal and omnipresent, is hidden and pervades all things.' (*Mahanirvana Tantra*)

ॐ मोहवर्जिताय नमः

Aum Mohavarjitaaya Namah

Salutations to the one devoid of delusions

Pure consciousness is all-knowing. It sifts illusion from reality and severs us from the bondage of desire by making us aware that identifying ourselves with our physical body is a false perception—that the true self transcends both the physical and emotional, and dwells, unfettered, as a rich experience.

ॐ वक्रतुंडाय नमः
Aum Vakratundaaya Namah

Salutations to the one with the curved trunk

The curved trunk is symbolic of active rather than passive energy. The more energy flows, the more it refines itself. The curved trunk has also been likened to the symbol Aum, which encompasses the whole universe and transcends the limits of time and space.

ॐ शूर्पकर्णाय नमः
Aum Shoorpakarnaaya Namah

Salutations to the one with ears like a winnowing basket

Ganesha's elephant ears have been likened to a winnowing basket. Just as the winnowing basket sifts the grain from the chaff, so also do Ganesha's ears filter out those sounds which are unnecessary and undesirable and draw and retain only those which are in consonance with the inner being. The large ears also symbolize Ganesha's ability to listen to all supplications.

ॐ परमाय नमः

Aum Paramaaya Namah

Salutations to the Absolute

Ganesha is a symbol of the *paraa shakti*, the supreme energy, that which is neither tangible nor perceived; the *summum bonum*, the highest good, beyond even the perfect and beyond the complete.

ॐ योगीशाय नमः

Aum Yogeeshaaya Namah

Salutations to the one able to unify all levels of energy

This aspect of Ganesha explores all the realms of the play of energy in the unified cosmic consciousness. He represents that power which aligns cosmic energy with those that exist at all three levels—the gross, the astral and the subtle.

ॐ योगधाम्ने नमः

Aum Yogadhaamney Namah

Salutations to the light of the glory of the universe

As Ganesha aligns the play of energies in the unified field of cosmic consciousness, he reflects the glory of the light of the universe. He is the ultimate yogi.

ॐ उमासुताय नमः
Aum Umasutaaya Namah

Salutations to the son of Uma

The sound *ooo* represents emotional kinetic energy; *mnnn* represents the higher consciousness. The two together represent the fusion of male and female energies. Ganesha was born of the union of physical energy and intellectual energy, i.e. the union of Parvati who is hailed as the mother of all creation and Shiva, who is pure consciousness.

ॐ आपद्धन्त्रे नमः
Aum Aapaddhantrey Namah

Salutations to the neutralizer of calamities

Once we understand the larger pattern of life then every crisis becomes a stepping stone towards the higher realization that we are essentially spiritual beings. As Aapaddhantrey, Ganesha bring this awareness to the fore, enabling us to analyse and therefore neutralize the perception of calamities.

ॐ एकदंताय नमः

Aum Ekadantaaya Namah

Salutations to the one with the single tusk

As Ekadanta, Ganesha vanquished the demons of vanity and arrogance. The single tusk represents single-mindedness.* The whole, perfect tusk represents truth and the unmanifest world. The broken, imperfect tusk represents the manifest world. The two together stand revealed as attributes of the same absolute. The single tusk also represents humility, for Ganesha broke his own tusk to destroy the demon Gajamukhasura.

In pre-Vedic times, the single tusk was seen as representing a plough, a stylus and also a weapon.

ॐ महाग्रीवाय नमः

Aum Mahaagreevaaya Namah

Salutations to the large-throated one

The throat is physically located between the mind and the heart and represents the unification of emotion and intellect. Ganesha's large throat symbolizes his ability to absorb experiences growing out of emotion and the intellect.

ॐ शरण्याय नमः
Aum Sharanyaaya Namah

Salutations to the one who gives refuge

Ganesha, with his qualities of immense benevolence and compassion, never refuses the seeker's plea for protection. When invoked with total surrender, he is quick to respond.

ॐ सिद्धसेनाय नमः
Aum Siddhasenaaya Namah

Salutations to the army of divine beings

Ganesha is the energy who cleanses, revitalizes and refines our cellular structure continuously. In the microcosm of our bodies, the cells are the counterpart of the celestial hosts. Ganesha regenerates all that is positive and helps us to evolve and become accomplished, divine beings.

ॐ सिद्धवेदाय नमः
Aum Siddhavedaaya Namah

**Salutations to the one who has assimilated
the wisdom of the *Vedas***

The *Vedas* impart guidance on how to conduct ourselves
and to obtain the maximum experience out of our
physical existence, so as to try and live a perfect life.
Ganesha is symbolic of one who has imbibed and
assimilated this wisdom. Moreover, he reveals the correct
way of life to us.

ॐ करुणाय नमः
Aum Karunaaya Namah

Salutations to the compassionate one

True knowledge, i.e. the realization of one's spiritual self, leads to immense and deep calmness. It generates purity of the heart by transcending the lower emotions which are replaced by compassion, mercy and love.

ॐ सिद्धाय नमः

Aum Siddhaaya Namah

ॐ सिद्धिविनायकाय नमः

Aum Siddhivinaayakaaya Namah

Salutations to the perfected one

The Siddhi Vinayak image of Ganesha has his trunk turned to his right. Lord Vishnu prayed to this image of Ganesha before his fight with the demons Madhu and Kaitabha to achieve strength to vanquish them.

ॐ भगवते नमः

Aum Bhagavatey Namah

Salutations to the lord almighty

Bhagvat is the supreme life force, the divine supreme potential in all forms which commands the unified field of cosmic energy. 'He is himself this universe, he is whatever is, has been and shall be.' (*Rig Veda*)

ॐ अव्यग्राय नमः

Aum Avyagraaya Namah

Salutations to the unruffled one

Ganesha is praised as the one who has attained stillness
of mind, as the one who can maintain equilibrium when
faced with the tantalizing kaleidoscope of illusion.

ॐ विकटाय नमः

Aum Vikataaya Namah

Salutations to the one with the gigantic form

Outward form is not necessarily a reflection of the inner state of beauty or spirituality. For personal growth we have to look beyond the physical. To reach the essence of a being we have to be aware of the many layers which could be concealing and thereby protecting a priceless gem.

ॐ कपिलाय नमः

Aum Kapilaaya Namah

Salutations to the tawny-coloured one

This refers to the youthful glowing complexion of
Ganesha. A healthy root chakra can be clairvoyantly seen
as having a golden centre with four red petals which
denote vitality and glowing health.

ॐ ढुढिराजाय नमः
Aum Dhundhiraajaaya Namah

Salutations to the neutralizer of evil forces

Dhundhiraja is a special form of Ganesha, very popular in Varanasi, revered in order to remove obstacles in the worship of Vishwanath (Lord Shiva). In other parts of India, Dhundhiraja Ganesha is seen as a great destroyer of evil forces. Images of Ganesha are also installed in accident-prone areas and at the dead-ends of roads.

ॐ उग्राय नमः
Aum Ugraaya Namah

Salutations to the one imbued with active force

Ganesha is that fierce life force which when activated propels us towards higher ambitions and accomplishments. When invoked with sincerity he motivates us towards achieving a profound and fulfilling completeness.

ॐ भीमोदराय नमः

Aum Bheemodaraaya Namah

Salutations to the one with the large abdomen

In this form, Ganesha overcame unjust, vicious anger.
The story of Ganesha and Kubera, (see Introduction
pp. 17–18), illustrates beautifully how Ganesha is not
appeased by wealth alone. The large abdomen is also
symbolic of the sorrows of the universe which Ganesha
swallows, thereby protecting it.

ॐ शुभाय नम:

Aum Shubhaaya Namah

Salutations to the auspicious one

A particular moment, or hour or day is considered
auspicious when there is a confluence of time, space and
energy in perfect balance. Born of pure refined energy,
Ganesha himself is symbolic of that confluence.

ॐ गणाद्यक्षाय नमः
Aum Ganaadhyakshaaya Namah

Salutations to the lord of the celestial hordes

Ganesha is the governor of the cellular system in every life form. He is all-pervasive, all-knowing, comprehensive energy. He is the lord of the spirit hordes, many of them malevolent. As their lord, he prevents them from interfering in the physical world.

ॐ गणेशाय नमः

Aum Ganeshaaya Namah

Salutations to the lord of the celestial hordes

Ganesha is the lord of all things, the different aspects of the One. He is the guarantor of success in all ventures, he gives knowledge to the seeker of wisdom, prosperity to those who seek worldly gain, progeny to the childless and blesses the path towards liberation.

ॐ गणाराध्याय नमः
Aum Ganaaraadhyaaya Namah

Salutations to the one worshipped by the celestial hordes

Prayers to the Divine Being need to be offered with total surrender. The true devotee prays with the entirety of his or her being—the physical self through ritual, the emotional self through faith and by being receptive at the sensory level.

ॐ गणनायकाय नमः
Aum Gananaayakaaya Namah

Salutations to the leader of the celestial hordes

Ganesha is the leader of every being of energy. He is the leader who guides every energy in the universe, the leader of the countless manifestations of the life force.

ॐ ज्योति:स्वरूपाय नम:

Aum Jyotihsvaroopaaya Namah

Salutations to the one who is light itself

Light reveals. As light itself, Ganesha reveals that precious knowledge which emerges through the experience of life. He illumines the seeker's path towards the source, the true centre, the inner being.

ॐ भूतात्मने नमः
Aum Bhootaatmaney Namah

Salutations to the eternal soul

As Bhootaatma, Ganesha represents everything that exists
in all the five elements. He is the very soul of the universe,
holy, eternal and aware of the cycle of time.

ॐ धूम्रकेतवे नमः
Aum Dhoomraketavey Namah

Salutations to the smoke-coloured one

Dhoomraketu is a comet, a mass of dust with a very bright tail. Ganesha helps destroy confusion in the minds of humans and helps overcome pride and egotism by seeing through the cloud of misconception created by it.

ॐ अनुकूलाय नमः
Aum Anukoolaaya Namah

Salutations to the one who is favourable for all

Ganesha is revered and loved by all—humans and celestials alike. He is invoked for material prosperity, better awareness, the expansion of consciousness, rich harvests and successful undertakings. The elephant-headed deity is worshipped not only in India but in Tibet, Central Asia, Mongolia and as far east as Japan.

ॐ कुमारगुरवे नमः
Aum Kumaaraguravey Namah

Salutations to the teacher of Kumar

Kumar, also known as Kartikeya, is Shiva's younger son.
Revered as the teacher of his younger brother, Ganesha
is associated with the first step of acquiring knowledge.
Traditionally, the mantra *Aum Ganeshaaya Namah* was
written or chanted during the initiation into education.

ॐ आनंदाय नमः

Aum Aanandaaya Namah

Salutations to the blissful one

'When division of subject and object created by ignorance is eliminated by enlightenment, there remains only the intrinsic, all-pervading bliss that is one and without a second.' (*Taittiriya Upanishad*)

ॐ हेरंबाय नमः

Aum Herambaaya Namah

Salutations to the beloved of his mother

As the beloved of Amba, his mother, Ganesha is represented as a five-headed deity and the protector of the weak. He protects us from excesses and overindulgence in appeasing the five senses. This aspect of Ganesha is sometimes invoked in the course of tantric practices.

ॐ वेदस्तुताय नमः
Aum Vedastutaaya Namah

**Salutations to the one who has knowledge
of all knowledge**

Knowledge of the unified field of energy is contained
and praised in the *Vedas*. Ganesha can redeem that
knowledge and express it. As such he is symbolic of the
pure expression of the *Vedas*.

ॐ नागयज्ञोपवीतिने नमः
Aum Naagayagyopaveetiney Namah

Salutations to the one who wears the snake as the sacred thread

The sacred thread is worn as a mark of initiation into education. The sacred thread also symbolizes flowing energy, emphasizing the fact that static energy is of no use until it is mobilized. The snake symbolizes the ascension of latent energy from the base of the spine to the crown. On a more earthly level, the snake is symbolic of lust. By tying the snake around his belly, Ganesha symbolizes the one who has conquered physicality.

ॐ दुर्धर्षाय नमः

Aum Durdharshaaya Namah

Salutations to the indomitable one

Ganesha is symbolic of the power of good energy which has been harnessed and refined. The force of this good energy is invincible.

ॐ बालदूर्वांकुरप्रियाय नमः

Aum Baaladoorvankurapriyaaya Namah

**Salutations to the one who is fond of the
tender shoots of *durvaa* grass**

Long before Ganesha was assimilated into the Hindu
pantheon, he was worshipped by farmers as a symbol of
fertility and prosperity. The tender shoots of durvaa grass,
which are traditionally offered to Ganesha, represent
both fertility and prosperity.

ॐ भालचंद्राय नमः
Aum Bhaalachandraaya Namah

Salutations to the one who wears the moon on his forehead

According to mythology, when Ganesha went to destroy Vighnaasura, the demon of obstacles, the various gods equipped him with their individual powers. The cresent moon was given to Ganesha by his father Shiva. The moon symbolizes the pot of nectar given by the gods to Shiva, to make him end his austerities after the death of Sati. As Bhaalachandra, Ganesha is adorned with Shiva's blessing.

ॐ विश्वधात्रे नमः

Aum Vishvadhaatrey Namah

Salutations to the one who nurtures the universe

The word *dhaatri* means to nurse or nurture. As nurturer of the universe, Ganesha enables the natural, free flow of energy by removing obstacles. The more good energy flows, the more good it generates.

ॐ शिवपुत्राय नमः

Aum Shivaputraaya Namah

Salutations to the son of Shiva

Shiva is acknowledged as the destroyer of ignorance. He is associated with the higher consciousness which has refined itself after destroying the demons of the lower emotions. Ganesha was born of the brilliance of Shiva's cosmic consciousness.

ॐ विनायकाय नमः
Aum Vinaayakaaya Namah

Salutations to the great leader

As Vinayaka, Ganesha is invoked as the great leader, the leader with special qualities, the one without blemish, the one who is the most powerful and the one whose energies are innately benign. He is depicted as red in colour, with four arms. In one hand he holds a *pasa* or noose, symbolic of binding love and in another he holds an axe symbolic of the cutting away of wrong attachments. His third hand holds a laddoo, the fourth bestows blessings.

ॐ लीलासेविताय नमः
Aum Leelaasevitaaya Namah

**Salutations to the one who is worshipped by
the play of cosmic energies**

Leela means the play of cosmic energies, the cosmic dance,
the fantastic and alluring web of illusion. Ganesha is
present at all levels of consciousness; as Leelasevita he
saves us from falling deeper into the trap of illusion, into
the realm of *maya*.

ॐ पूर्णाय नमः

Aum Poornaaya Namah

Salutations to the complete one

'The Supreme Being is complete and it is absolute. Creation, which emerges from the Supreme Being is also complete. Take away that which has emerged, the remainder will still be complete. Peace be to all.' (*Isha Upanishad*)

ॐ परमसुंदराय नमः
Aum Paramasundaraaya Namah

Salutations to the most beautiful one

Born of the brilliance of Shiva's mental energy, Ganesha reflects that radiance. Shiva is pure consciousness. Ganesha's refined mass of energy makes him Paramasundara—the most brilliant and the most beautiful, the one who radiates effulgence.

ॐ विघ्नांधकाराय नमः

Aum Vighnaandhakaaraaya Namah

Salutations to the one who is like darkness to obstacles

The strength of Ganesha's positive energy obliterates obstacles. When invoked, he leads us from the darkness of ignorance and obstacles into the light of knowledge.

ॐ सिंदूरवरदाय नमः

Aum Sindooravaradaaya Namah

Salutations to the bestower of prosperity and happiness

Sindoor or vermilion is mercury oxide. Red is also the colour of vitality. Sindoor is traditionally worn on the forehead for better application of the finer intellect represented by the planet Mercury. As Sindooravardana, Ganesha also blesses the union of man and woman in marriage.

ॐ नित्याय नमः
Aum Nityaaya Namah

Salutations to the imperishable one

Ganesha symbolizes that which is constant, everlasting, imperishable and ever-present.

ॐ विभवे नमः

Aum Vibhavey Namah

Salutations to the omnipresent one

Ganesha is omnipresent, ebullient, opulent energy.
'This self in the lord of all beings as all spokes converge
together in the hub, all things, all gods, all men, all lives,
all bodies converge together in that self.' (*Chandogya
Upanishad*)

ॐ प्रथमपूजिताय नमः

Aum Prathamapoojitaaya Namah

Salutations to the one who is worshipped first

It is considered auspicious to invoke Ganesha with the mantra *Aum Shree Ganeshaaya Namah* at the beginning of any venture. As one who nourishes the very basis of our existence, he also makes us receptive to divine energy. His blessings protect us and sensitize us towards higher goals.

ॐ दिव्यपादाब्जाय नमः

Aum Divyapaadaabjaaya Namah

Salutations to the divine lotus feet

The entry point of divine energy is the crown chakra. This divine energy flows through the body and out of the feet. By connecting ourselves to the benevolent energy emanating from Ganesha's lotus-like feet, we become more capable of assimilating pure blessings.

ॐ भक्तमंदराय नम:

Aum Bhaktamandaraaya Namah

Salutations to the abode of the devotee

For the *bhakta* or devotee, Ganesha is like Mount Mandara, which was used as the churning rod in the myth of the churning of the ocean. This churning brought forth poison and nectar, as well as the goddess Lakshmi, the cow Kamadhenu and the Kalpavriksha tree. Mount Mandara is therefore symbolic of the rod which separates good from evil. Likewise, a prayer to Ganesha brings forth success and fulfils wishes.

ॐ शूरमहाय नमः
Aum Shooramahaaya Namah

Salutations to the one with the lustre of a warrior

As Shooramaha, Ganesha represents the strength of one who is brave and valiant. He also represents the glory of the conquest of good over evil. He reflects the glory and radiance of the victor, of the one who has achieved and accomplished those higher goals towards which Ganesha takes us.

ॐ रत्नसिंहासनाय नमः

Aum Ratnasinghaasanaaya Namah

Salutations to the one seated on the bejewelled throne

Clear, pure energy has all the seven colours of the spectrum. Ganesha sits on the jewelled throne imbued with the colours of many brilliant energies.

ॐ मणिकुंडलमंडिताय नमः
Aum Manikundalamanditaaya Namah

**Salutations to the one adorned with
jewelled earrings**

The ear lobes contain nerve-endings directly connected
to the brain. Piercing the lobes connects the left brain to
the right brain, thus fusing intuition with reasoning. As
a shape, that which is *kund* (round) is stronger, for it is
continuous. In this epithet, Ganesha is a symbol of one
who is adorned with orbs of integrated energy.

ॐ भक्तकल्याणाय नम:

Aum Bhaktakalyaanaaya Namah

Salutations to the one who seeks the welfare of the devotee

This epithet invokes Ganesha as the auspicious energy which is devoted to the welfare of the devotee. When invoked, Ganesha responds and clears the way for the improvement of the devotee at every level.

ॐ गजास्याय नम:

Aum Gajaasyaaya Namah

Salutations to the elephant-headed one

The large but gentle elephant is the embodiment of goodness and virtue. It is loyal and affectionate. Its size belies its non-violent nature; it is therefore not viewed with fear. However, when it is provoked, the elephant can be both powerful and violently destructive.

ॐ कल्यानगुरवे नमः
Aum Kalyaanaguravey Namah

Salutations to the benevolent master

The guru is the one who dispels darkness, ignorance and negativity and leads us to light. As Kalyaanaguru, Ganesha is the benevolent master who possesses the rare quality of teaching and giving only that which is good and benevolent.

ॐ सहस्त्रशीर्ष्णे नमः
Aum Sahastrasheershney Namah

Salutations to the thousand-headed one

This epithet refers to the 1000 petals of the crown chakra or the *sahastraar chakra*. When all the petals of this chakra are fully enlightened, it symbolizes the containment of the light of complete knowledge. The crown chakra is the pure dimension where the interplay between energy and consciousness happens at a transcendental level.

ॐ महागणपतये नमः
Aum Mahaaganapatayey Namah

Salutations to the great lord of the heavenly hosts

As Mahaganapati, Ganesha symbolizes Aum, which is the sound vibration of the entire cosmos. The sound *aaa* denotes procreative or physical energy; *ooo* denotes emotional, kinetic energy; *mnnn* denotes the higher consciousness and psycho-spiritual energy. If we connect to the sound within while chanting, then with the sound 'a' we will feel the latent energy stimulating the base of the spine. The sound 'u' emanates from the heart, while *mnnn* resonates in the nimbus. The resonance created by the three syllables, which are uttered in a continuous flow as *Omn* or *Aum*, represents the entire cosmos.

Ganesha Mantras

These are the three mantras frequently used to invoke Ganesha. These, too, may be chanted 108 times.

ॐ श्री गणेशाय नम:

Aum Shree Ganeshaaya Namah
Salutations to Lord Ganesha

ॐ गं गणपतये नम:

Aum Gangm Ganapatayey Namah
Salutations to the lord of all celestial energy beings

Ganesha Gayatri

ॐ तत्पुरुषाय विद्महे वक्रतुण्डाय धीमहि तन्नो दन्ति: प्रचोदयात्

Aum Tatpurushaya Vidmahey Vakratundaya Dheemahi Tanno Dantih Prachodayat.
Salutations to the one with the curved trunk, the source of all intelligence, who may inspire and guide me towards the light of knowledge.

About the Author

Ashima Singh is a pranic healer-teacher and former media person based in New Delhi who has conducted self-awareness and personal growth workshops in many countries. She has studied the religious philosophy, art and literature of many cultures in her quest to relate to the energy force that binds all humanity. She imparts to this book her keen awareness and knowledge of this energy force and talks about how it can have a positive effect on our lives.